Marie Stopes
and Birth Control

Marie Stopes in 1914.

Pioneers of Science and Discovery

Marie Stopes
and Birth Control

Harry Verdon Stopes-Roe
with
Ian Scott

PRIORY PRESS LIMITED

Other Books in this Series

SBN 85078 115 9

Copyright by H. V. Stopes-Roe
First Published in 1974 by
Priory Press Ltd., 101 Grays Inn Road, London WC1.
Text set in 12/14 pt. Photon Baskerville, printed by
photolithography and bound in Great Britain at
The Pitman Press, Bath.

Contents

Illustrations

"Arrest them all-- The laws of decency must be respected!"

1 *Sex Before Stopes*

Marie Stopes believed in the right of every woman to equality and joy in marriage; sexual intercourse was spiritually ennobling and physically good. She held a rather extreme romantic view, and today it sometimes seems a little overstated, but we must remember that she was reacting against a moral viewpoint quite alien to us.

It is hard for us to get a realistic impression of the sexual attitudes of the middle classes towards the end of the last century. However, in order to understand how great was Marie Stopes's achievement and how great the revolution in attitudes which she helped to bring about, we must try to get into the mind of an average, respectable Victorian, and to feel the horror that he or she felt about sex.

The Victorian attitude to sex was quite unique in its strength and duration. With few exceptions, people in all other ages had thought of sex as part and parcel of everyday life. They behaved and talked about sex quite freely. The Victorian middle classes, however, came to believe that anything to do with sex was shameful, disgusting and even a betrayal of God. Sex for Victorian women was a necessary evil, to be suffered without pleasure. It was their duty to satisfy their husbands and to become mothers. If they were "unfortunate" enough to enjoy it they felt ashamed. To be a parent was a wonderful thing, but the means to that end were considered repugnant to refined tastes.

This attitude had far-reaching effects throughout Victorian society and showed itself in behaviour, language, literature, dress and even politics. In their search for respectability and refinement, Victorians

Opposite top An early twentieth century cartoon ridiculing the extremes reached by the Victorians' search for respectability and decency.

Opposite bottom Women's fashions reflected the moral attitudes of the Victorians. Full, long dresses prevented even a glimpse of a women's ankle, let alone a look at her legs—that would have been most improper!

9

tried to keep sex out of sight, out of earshot and out of mind. It should take place in the dark, in secret and in absolute silence. It should be banned from conversation, and so it was, to such an extent that in January, 1851, the *Economist* considered that "the general tone of morals in the middle and higher classes has unquestionably become higher and purer in the last generation. Language which was common in our fathers' days would not be tolerated now. A higher sense, both of duty and of decency, has taken possession of all ranks."

The attack on sex was vigorously backed up by churchmen, by doctors who promised disease and madness to those who broke the rules, by libraries which refused to handle any book which carried even the slightest reference to sex, and by Queen Victoria herself who on more than one occasion vetoed the appointment to high office of certain men of whom she disapproved on moral grounds.

Above left Henry Labouchère (1831–1912) and Sir Charles Dilke (1843–1911), two politicians whose "immoral" behaviour had caused Queen Victoria to stop them holding any high political posts that brought them into contact with her. Labouchère had lived for a time with an actress before marrying her. Dilke's career was ruined by his involvement in a spectacular divorce case.

If someone suggested today that the best way to reduce hunger in the world would be to kill off all the hungry, or that a good way to control population would be to slaughter a set number of children every month, most people would disagree quite violently. If, on top of that, it was agreed that killing hungry people or children should also be *enjoyable*, people would be horrified. They would "know" without doubt that this was wrong.

So it was with the Victorians and the idea that sex should be enjoyed. The Victorians "knew" that the ideas that Marie Stopes later wrote about were wrong and shocking. At the height of her career as a social reformer in the 1920s (only fifty years ago) Marie was thought of by many people, not just as a misguided crank, but as a really evil influence. We now believe that the Victorians were quite wrong about this and, equally, we are confident that our views on killing hungry people and young children are right.

Marie Stopes brought into the open the taboo subject of sex, surrounded as it was by ignorance and disgust, fear and shame, and above all by a wall of silence. (No words existed which were polite enough to be used in mixed company.) She argued that not only should it be talked about widely and freely but it should be enjoyed: "So many people," she wrote in her best-seller, *Married Love*, "are now born and bred in artificial and false surroundings, that even the elementary fact that the acts of love should be *joyous* is unknown to them." Such a powerful means of giving and receiving pleasure ought to be a way of drawing two people closer together. Marie believed that sex was a beautiful experience, to be enjoyed and valued.

She was not slow to realize that birth control must follow. Indeed, this was to be the focus of her most famous battles. The very idea of birth control by mechanical interference with the sex act seemed quite outrageous and was generally condemned on both moral and religious grounds. In separating the physical side of sex from its function of producing children, the argument ran, it encouraged lust and immorality, selfishness and lack of self control.

In 1908 the Lambeth Conference of Bishops called upon "all Christian people to discountenance the use of all artificial means of restriction [of the family] as demoralizing to character and hostile to national welfare." It declared that "deliberate tampering with nascent life is repulsive to Christian morality." As such it was, like abortion, a variety of murder. The 1920 Lambeth Conference stated that contraception "encourages married people in the deliberate cultivation of sexual union as an end in itself."

Doctors, too, objected to birth control. They claimed that it led to sterility and disease. Finally, a curious double standard of morality existed at the turn of the century which admitted that contraception, like prostitution, was used correctly by the rich, but should be denied to the poor (who stood in much greater need of contraception).

The arguments for birth control are complex:
(1) it is a foundation for the pure enjoyment of sex;
(2) it is needed to prevent overpopulation;
(3) it is needed to lessen the misery of the poor, by releasing them from endless pregnancies;
(4) it has implications for the race, and for race improvements.

Our attitudes on each one of these points are very different from those current in the early part of this century.

Consider overpopulation. For us, the "population explosion" is an obvious and pressing problem, and birth control is an obvious part of the answer. People have begun to understand its full significance only over the last few decades. Certainly, the possibility of overpopulation had been recognized as early as the eighteenth century, but it was not central to the controversies in the 1920s about birth control—and it played no part in Marie Stopes's thought at that time.

Right A nineteenth century French drawing of syphilis in its secondary stage. The disease was regarded by many people as just punishment for immoral behaviour.

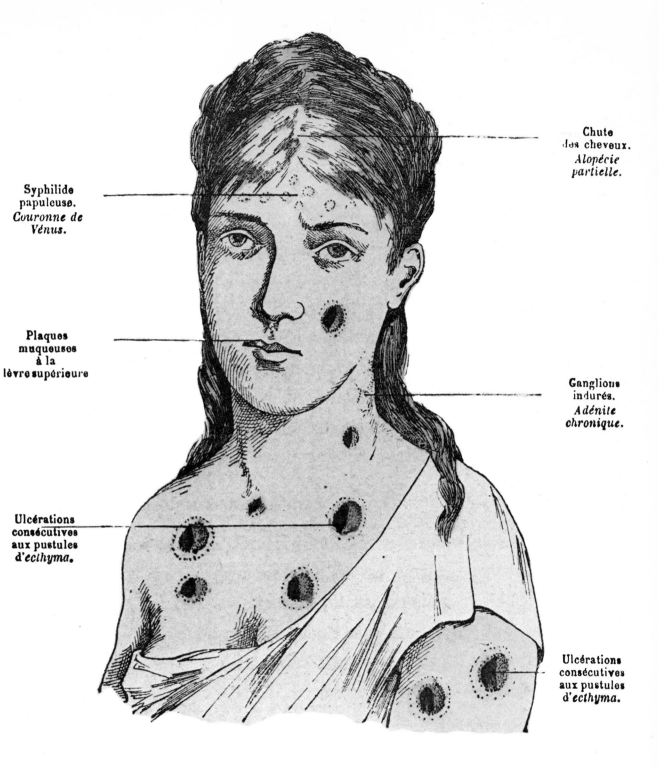

Chute
des cheveux.
*Alopécie
partielle.*

Syphilide
papuleuse.
*Couronne de
Vénus.*

Plaques
muqueuses
à la
lèvre supérieure

Ganglions
indurés.
*Adénite
chronique.*

Ulcérations
consécutives
aux pustules
d'*ecthyma.*

Ulcérations
consécutives
aux pustules
d'*ecthyma.*

13

Right Mrs. Annie Besant (1847–1933), one of the leaders of the birth control or neo-Malthusian movement of the late nineteenth century. (Thomas Malthus (1766–1834) was an economist at Cambridge University who argued that unless population was kept down there would come a time when it would no longer be possible to find food for it. He argued for "moral restraint"—that is, no marriage and no sex—as the answer to this problem. Neo-Malthusians favoured methods of contraception.)

Left Charles Bradlaugh (1833–91) being ejected from the House of Commons in 1880 after his right, as an atheist, to take the oath of office was denied. Bradlaugh believed, with Annie Besant (*above right*), that families should be limited and population controlled and he supported her campaign to teach people, especially the poor, methods of contraception.

Concern with the welfare of the poor was a major interest of reformers in the nineteenth century. Some of the great social reformers of that time were also firm supporters of birth control. A concern for the poor was shared by people of many religious views, but the idea of helping them to limit their families was taboo. To be able to think in terms of birth control at all in the religious and social atmosphere of the time required a free-thinking (non-Christian) mind, and most of these early reformers were not members of a church.

One such, Charles Bradlaugh, was born in 1833, just before Victoria became queen. The son of a solicitor's clerk, he became an atheist, and had to leave home at an early age. Largely self-taught, he soon made a reputation as a radical speaker. He advocated such diverse things as free speech and birth control, and became one of the most controversial Members of Parliament of his day.

In 1876 he published a physiological treatise, *Fruits of Philosophy*, with Mrs. Annie Besant, another free-thinker, who had left home as a result of ill-treatment by her husband, a clergyman, and had lost her Christian faith. They were prosecuted for publishing an obscene book and found guilty but, having won an appeal on a technicality, they promptly sued the police for the return of the confiscated copies and began to sell them once more. Mrs. Besant later wrote a book called *The Law of Population* which she dedicated to "the poor in great cities and agricultural districts, dwellers in stifling court or crowded hovel, in the hope that it may point out a path from poverty, and make easier the life of British mothers." It described all the methods of contraception then in use and eventually sold more than 175,000 copies.

There were great fighters in the nineteenth century, both for the human value of sex and for birth control in particular. Robert Owen, another free-thinker, said, "Chastity, sexual intercourse *with* affection. Prostitution, sexual intercourse *without* affection."

Marie Stopes's concern with race improvement was a particularly thorny problem. It was widely believed that a high birth rate proved the virility of the race; any effort to curb the birth rate would lead to a catastrophic decline in the population. The fact that half of the intending army recruits in York, Leeds and Sheffield during the Boer War were rejected on medical grounds, while proving a shock to the Edwardians, did little to dispel this view. Marie Stopes's motto was "Babies in the right place." It was not, in the view of the general public, the obvious solution to the problem of producing a healthier population.

It is against this background that her famous book *Married Love* was written. Nowadays it seems very tame, rather romantic and idealized, and the sort of thing that might be published in any woman's magazine. But in 1918 it was a bombshell.

Below Marie's father, Henry Stopes (1852–1902), brewer's engineer and architect who spent much of his spare studying and searching for fossils. He particularly interested in finding remai early man.

2 *A Strict Upbringing*

Marie Stopes was born in Edinburgh, her mother's home town, on 15th October, 1880. Six weeks later the family moved to a house in South London.

Her father, Henry Stopes, came from an Essex family of Quakers with a brewing business in Colchester, although he himself practised as a brewers' engineer and architect with offices in London. They lived, during most of Marie's childhood, in an Elizabethan house in Swanscombe, near Dartford in Kent. Here Henry could indulge his passion for palaeontology—the study of extinct animals and plants. He had chosen Swanscombe because he

Below The front cover of one book and the title page of another written by Henry Stopes on brewing.

BARLEY

AND THE

BEER DUTY

WITH ILLUSTRATION.

H. STOPES.

PRICE ONE SHILLING.

LONDON:
W. A. May, "The Mark Lane Express,"
1, Essex Street, Strand, W.C.
— 1901. —

MALT AND MALTING.

BY

H. STOPES.

PNEUMATIC MALTHOUSE, YEOVIL.

LONDON:
F. W. LYON,
BREWERS' JOURNAL OFFICE, EASTCHEAP BUILDINGS, E.C.

1885.

thought that the brick earth and gravels in the area would be rich in the remains of prehistoric man. Just how right he was he never knew. Not until some years after his death were skull fragments found there of what became known as Swanscombe Man, now looked upon as the first representatives found of *Homo Sapiens*, our own species of man.

Marie's mother, Charlotte Carmichael, came from a Scottish Calvinist background. A deeply intellectual woman, she was one of the first women to attend Edinburgh University, studying English literature and philosophy. In all, she wrote eight books, including studies on William Shakespeare and Francis Bacon. She was, like her husband, concerned about the rights of women and, in particular, the promotion of "rational dress" for women. At a time when most women devoted themselves entirely to domestic matters, this helped to make her a very unusual woman. Marie found her a rather cold mother and seems to have had very little emotional support from

Below Rational dress for women. In the 1880s there was a movement away from the awkward fashions of the previous twenty or thirty years and towards a more sensible way of dressing that would let women move about more freely.

her. She could only remember having been praised by her once, late in life and very indirectly. When Marie's only surviving child (the author) was born Charlotte said to her: "A fine child, but not as handsome as mine."

Charlotte Stopes was preoccupied with her daughter's intellectual development from a very early age. When Marie was two months old her mother wrote in her diary that "baby has shewn great intellectual development. . ." By the time Marie was five she was trying to teach her Latin and Greek, but with little success. Thereafter she stuck to reading and writing.

Her mother's rather stern Calvinism, with its emphasis on hellfire and a strict upbringing, was the main religious influence in Marie's early life. In fact, Marie seems as a child to have worried greatly about sin and the need for redemption. As a mature woman she could still vividly remember her feelings at the age of six or seven. "My manifold sins had been made very evident to me and I felt that if only I were a better girl I

Below left Charlotte Stopes (1841–1929), Marie's mother and a great supporter of the rational dress movement.

Below right Marie Stopes in December 1887, aged 7 years and 1½ months

Left Marie and her younger sister Winnie as children

should feel the actual floods of the Blood of Jesus which would purify me." She goes on: "I felt that I must try to be converted in such a way that I really could see and feel these things. I remember placing myself at the foot of a long flight of stairs at the bottom of which was a sheepskin mat, dyed crimson, and I rubbed myself in the crimson wool of the mat and shut my eyes and tried to picture the stream of the Blood of the Lamb cascading down the stairs over me, purifying me and taking away my manifold sins."

But her mother was not the only influence in the girl's early life. Marie spent a lot of time with her father, too. In Swanscombe, Henry could take her with him on his searches for prehistoric stone tools. Any flint which bore the slightest trace of human working would be collected. Later, with Marie's eager help, they were sorted and labelled. Sometimes the whole family, would go on these expeditions.

Not until she was twelve was Marie sent to school. When she arrived at St. George's School in Edin-

Above St. George's School, Edinburgh where Marie went from 1892 for two years.

burgh, her education had been very unbalanced. She knew more about palaeontology and one or two other subjects than other girls of her age, but she was way behind in most subjects. It humiliated her to find herself in a class of girls several years younger than herself. The two years she stayed at St. George's were a constant struggle to catch up, a struggle that she never completely won.

When she was fourteen, Marie was sent to the North London Collegiate School. At first she did little better than at St. George's. Indeed, the headmistress and chemistry mistress were the only two of her teachers to regard her as anything special. Chemistry was Marie's best subject. Once, when the chemistry mistress fell ill, Marie took over the teaching of the class. With the encouragement and special tuition of Miss Aitken, the chemistry mistress, she did outstandingly well in this subject and won a leaving scholarship in science.

Marie's parents and her headmistress advised her

to go to a women's college, but instead she enrolled at University College, London, in the Faculty of Science. With unbounded confidence in her intellectual ability she took the unprecedented step of asking permission to start at once on the honours course. Although she was refused, she cannot have been completely surprised. However, a more sympathetic approach by the Professor of Botany persuaded her to change to botany as her main subject, with chemistry second. At the end of her first year she won the Gold Medal in botany and was second in her class in zoology.

What, one wonders, would she have made of her

Above University College, London, were Marie worked for her Bachelor of Science degree which she got with first class honours in botany and geology in 1902.

life if her chemistry teachers at University College had let her do as she asked? As it was, botany—or rather palaeobotany, for she managed to link her father's consuming interest in palaeontology with her career as a botanist—was to occupy the first twenty years of her adult life.

Due partly, perhaps, to those wretched years at St. George's when she had to struggle even to appear average, Marie seems to have felt it was not enough to do well, even exceptionally well. She had to attempt the apparently impossible. During her first year at University College, besides her normal classes during the day, she went to evening classes at Birkbeck College. She found that she could enter her name to sit for an honours degree as an external student on the basis of her evening classes. In doing so, provided she could learn enough in the time, she would be able to take the examination in a year instead of the usual three years.

At this period, Marie Stopes was still sexually immature. Apart from a rather one-sided relationship with a young man at University College, all of her emotional energies seem to have been directed towards her own sex. She became involved in several rather intense friendships with women, especially with an older woman who seems to have been an earlier teacher. While not unusual either then or now, this dependence on her own sex did hamper her emotional development and thus, when her first real attachment to a man occurred, she was less prepared for it than most girls of her age would have been.

Meanwhile, her parents, who had never been very close—Charlotte's lack of warmth made this unlikely—slowly drifted further apart. Henry spent more and more time away from home. In a letter to him Marie complained, "A birthday is not half a birthday without you—and this is the second I have had without you." Also his health was rapidly deteriorating. By the time Marie was due to sit her final examinations he was already dying of an internal disease. Not long before he died on 5th December, 1902, at the age of fifty, Marie learned that she had passed with double honours.

Henry's premature death was a shock to Charlotte from which she did not completely recover; the vigour of her earlier years was gone. In addition, the fact that Henry had left little money made the family's future rather precarious. All of this makes Marie's decision to go to Munich for further study, having gained her B.Sc. with honours, unexpected. It says a great deal about the singlemindedness with which she was always to pursue her various careers. Moreover, it was evidently a decision which produced a degree of friction between herself and her mother.

3 Marie Stopes the Scientist

Marie Stopes's life falls naturally into three phases, each of which lasted for roughly twenty years. The first was devoted to science, the second to social services and the third to poetry. She entered the first—the scientific—period from a position of immense strength. She needed a very great deal of strength and confidence to make her way in what was still overwhelmingly a male preserve, the field of scientific research.

She chose Munich as the university where she would complete her education and decided to work under Professor Goebel in the Botanical Institute, studying palaeobotany. The first problem was that, although women had been allowed to work in the Institute, and had even been awarded degrees in other faculties, the regulations of the university made it impossible for a woman to obtain a doctorate in botany. As things turned out, however, Professor Goebel, impressed by his student, himself removed this obstacle by having the rules changed.

The second problem was that all examinations, including the oral, had to be taken in German. Also, the oral exam took place in front of the whole university. This was a frightening prospect for someone who spoke very little German and who had always found it difficult to learn languages. Still, with characteristic doggedness, Marie set about learning the language and by the end of her stay in Munich was easily able to hold her own in the exam.

Marie's capacity for work was enormous. She was sometimes known to work for thirty hours at a stretch, not even stopping for meals. She fed herself with beef tea which she kept warm on a spirit stove close by. Her normal day in the laboratory, however, began at eight

Below Marie in Munich, where she studied for her Doctorate of Philosophy in botany in 1903 and 1904

in the morning and lasted twelve hours.

Given her lack of experience of men, and the fact that she was herself a foreigner in Munich, it is natural that she should have struck up a friendship with another foreigner, Professor Kuyiro Fujii, a Japanese botanist. Fujii was some years older than Marie and already married, although by the time they met his marriage was breaking up. The relationship quickly ripened. By the time Marie left Munich they were already writing to each other in affectionate terms and discussing the possibility of Fujii's visiting England to see her.

Marie's work at Munich was largely concerned with the fertilization of the cycads. This is an order of plants which has very few representatives surviving now, but which was of major importance over the period from about 250 million years to 100 million years ago. Their appearance is not unlike that of palms, though botanically they are quite different. On the basis of this work she was awarded her Ph.D. *magna cum laude*—"with great praise."

Much as she might have liked to stay in Munich, particularly in view of her growing friendship with Fujii, her work there was unpaid. Having gained her doctorate, she had to think about getting a proper job. She heard of an assistant lectureship which had fallen vacant at Manchester and posted her application for it before leaving Munich.

Marie was the first woman to lecture in the science faculty at Manchester, a distinction she owed in part to Professor Boyd Dawkins whom she had impressed with her enthusiasm while at University College. She seems to have settled into her new world remarkably quickly and made several friends among the staff.

At the age of twenty-four she had at last achieved a position in the scientific world, but had done so only by driving herself very hard. Marie was determined to make an international name for herself.

She now turned her attention to coal. The existence

Above This photograph, taken during Marie Stopes' Royal Society expedition to Japan in 1907, shows a group of cycads in the Botanical Gardens at Tokyo wrapped up for protection against the winter snows. Other plants of the group known as gymnosperms are shown *below*. (1) to (6) are conifers, well-known and plentiful. (7) is the fruit of the Gingko ("Maidenhair Tree"), now almost

or quite extinct in the wild, having been preserved for centuries in temple gardens in the East.

Below Examples of the huge group of plants known as angiosperms. *Left* the Purple Foxglove, *centre* Wheat and *right* Barley.

of a large number of mines around Manchester diverted her interest to this geological period—in which the cycads, subject of her Munich researches, had originated.

The Manchester period was a good time for her, both in her work and in her personal life. Not only did she make many friends, but her relationship with Professor Fujii deepened. He had managed to follow her from Munich and, although he had to live in London, they managed to meet occasionally and wrote frequent letters to each other. The letters which survive make it clear that one of the few things about Fujii that Marie Stopes could never accept was his atheism and rejection of a belief in an afterlife. She did her best to persuade him to believe otherwise, for she passionately believed that, far from diminishing religious faith, science simply confirmed a belief in God.

Fujii, of course, could not stay in England for ever. For one thing, his money was running out and he had a career of his own to pursue in Japan. However, before he left, they made plans to write and publish a scientific paper together. This was a project that was to take longer than Marie could have anticipated.

Meanwhile, Marie's agile mind was off on another tack—the origin of angiosperms. Angiosperms form the more recent of the two large groups of seed-bearing plants—those which flower. The others are the gymnosperms. The cycads and conifers (e.g. the fir, larch, pine, cedar, sequoia and cypress) are gymnosperms. Angiosperms are now by far the most common kind of plant. Even in thick pine forests or on moors covered in moss and bracken (which are neither angiosperms nor gymnosperms) angiosperms such as grass, brambles and a host of small plants still predominate. So the question of where the angiosperms came from was, and is, of vital importance. They originated during the Cretaceous Period—the geological period lasting from about 135

Opposite Photographs from the Japan expedition. *Top* The coolies who carried the tents, food and the rest of the camp equipment on an expedition into the jungle on Hokkaido, at breakfast one morning around the camp fire. *Bottom* River shallows showing some of the fossil-bearing nodules for which Marie Stopes was searching.

million to 65 million years ago. It occurred to Marie Stopes that, given certain conditions in the surrounding horizons, the existence of the type of fossil for which she was searching could be more or less predicted.

Her theory pointed to Hokkaido, the northernmost island of Japan, and to test it she wrote to Fujii (now back in Japan) explaining her theory and asking him to send her some likely rock samples. To her delight, the first sample contained such a fossil. The Royal Society was so impressed by her discovery that they gave her a grant to finance an expedition to Japan. This was the first time that they had ever sent a woman on such an expedition.

Her time in Japan was very busy indeed. Her search for fossils took her into the wildest parts of the country, and often to places where no Westerner had set foot before. On one trip she found what was then the earliest known angiosperm. The intervals between her trips were spent largely in Tokyo working with Professor Fujii on their joint paper.

However, not all of her work at this time was to do with palaeobotany. She was fascinated by the special theatre of Japan—the Nō plays. She and Professor

Below A Japanese Nō play in progress.

Marie Stopes with Kuyiro Fujii (1866–1952) (seated on her right), Professor Joji Sakurai (1858–1939) (standing on her left) and two friends on board ship shortly before she left Japan for Vancouver, Canada on her way back to England.

Reginald Ruggles Gates (1882–1962), the Canadian botanist who became Marie's first husband.

Sakurai, the Dean of the Imperial University, translated three of these plays into English for the first time. This is the first evidence of a literary talent which eventually led to her election to the Royal Society of Literature. Her interest in writing, particularly poetry, was to dominate her later years.

A powerful mind will create achievement out of anything and it may well be that the force driving her to formulate the theory which led to Japan was the desire to be close to her friend Fujii. Certainly their relationship was deep enough now for her to be thinking of marriage, and Fujii's first marriage had by then completely broken up and he was divorced. But this was not to be. Professor Fujii fell seriously ill and his convalescence was long and complicated, so that the prospect of marriage receded from both of their minds. Her position was further complicated by the fact that her grant from the Royal Society was rapidly running out and she had to make plans to return to England. Fujii saw her off from Yokohama.

Back in London Marie's work went on, and she seemed to be settling down to a lifetime devoted to science and spinsterhood. She had already been awarded a D.Sc. degree, becoming one of the youngest people to hold it in the country, and so could call herself Dr. Stopes. It was a style she insisted on keeping through both her marriages.

She travelled widely in the course of her work, both in Europe and North America. On a trip to the United States in 1911 she met Ruggles Gates, a Canadian botanist. They seem to have felt an immediate attraction for each other. With the unhappy affair with Fujii relatively fresh in her mind, Marie Stopes was cautious at first, but not so Gates. Within a week of their first meeting he proposed to her and they were married not long afterwards in Montreal.

Almost at once they moved to London and set up house in Hampstead. From the start there were problems in the marriage which sprang from the fact that her husband was impotent. The resultant strains were so great that the marriage soon broke up amid much recrimination on both sides.

One can begin to get a picture of Marie Stopes's emotional development up to this point. She was powerful in her intellect and also in her emotions. Her parents were hard, cold and demanding. She had a very close relationship with her father until his early death; perhaps he was himself an emotional man who was repressed. At no time did she have any emotional support from her mother—not even at this time of trouble.

She had a highly romantic and idealized relationship with a philosophically-minded Asian. Sex to her was of immense importance; but it was hedged by conventions and ideals. Her ideas of sex came more from what she felt in a mystical way, and from romantic art and literature, than from practical or scientific experience.

She knew her need for sexual fulfilment, though we can be fairly sure that up to this time there had been no real love-making. We can see the importance to her of her marriage, and so understand the impact of the catastrophe. We have some insight into her mind from letters she wrote to Aylmer Maude.

Maude, friend, translator and biographer of the Russian writer Leo Tolstoy, came first to know the Gates, and was then their lodger. He knew all about the breakdown of their marriage, and became Marie's confidant. She formed a very close and loving relationship with him, and they might have married if he had not been so much older. Maude wrote Marie's first biography in 1924. In a letter to him after two and a half years of the Gates marriage, she wrote commenting on the superficial harmony there sometimes was with Gates: "Real kisses would still matter to me immensely. . .If ever I kiss you, it must be with a piece of my soul—if my soul ever comes back to me again." This friendship lasted until Maude's death; he was

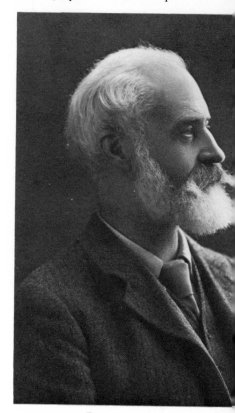

Below Aylmer Maude (1858–1938), friend and first biographer of Marie Stopes.

known as "Grandpa" to Marie's son, the young Harry Stopes-Roe.

In the end, she screwed up her courage and went to a solicitor to start proceedings for an annulment of her marriage on the grounds of non-consummation. It was 1914 and the marriage had lasted just three years.

To escape the unpleasantness, Marie spent the next few weeks camping in Northumberland on her own. She had long enjoyed the simplicity and solitude of life in a tent (there was her Japanese expedition, as well as another to Norway which had taken her inside the Arctic Circle, and many others less dramatic). Her love of this way of life always remained with her.

On her return to London in 1914 at the start of the First World War she resumed the work on coal which she had started in her Manchester days. This was now, in wartime, a project of national importance. With Dr. R. V. Wheeler she published a paper on the structure of coal, and another on its ingredients by herself. Both of these papers are, even today, considered to be of great importance by experts on coal.

Her interest in these scientific matters, on which she had already spent so much time and energy, went on for the rest of her life. But gradually, as she became attracted to other things, they tended to fall further into the background.

4 Married Love

Alone in her tent in Northumberland, Marie began slowly to work out her thoughts on sex and marriage. What she started at this time became, four years later, the basis of her famous book *Married Love*. Her purpose was to help married couples understand each other's physical and spiritual needs. As she wrote in *Married Love*, "It is never *easy* to make marriage a lovely thing; and it is an achievement beyond the powers of the selfish, or the mentally cowardly.

"Knowledge is needed and, as things are at present, knowledge is almost unobtainable by those who are most in want of it.

"The problems of the sex-life are infinitely complex, and for their solution urgently demand both sympathy and scientific research."

It was not just the break-up of her marriage which made her write the book, although it undoubtedly played a large part in doing so. Countless women before her had suffered marriages which were just as unhappy, but no woman before had been prompted by her experience to write a book on the subject of physical love.

What made her so different from other women? If we look closely at her life up to this period we can see two very significant strands of development which, combined in her unique character, can perhaps account for this difference.

The first of these factors was her longstanding interest in social questions and, in particular, the rights of women. This was an interest which she had inherited from both her parents. She was never a suffragette and did not actively campaign for votes for women, yet she was deeply concerned with the status of women, both social and legal, and was very con-

Opposite Marie Stopes in 1918, four years after her marriage to Ruggles Gates had been annulled.

scious that married women in particular were at a great disadvantage.

In a later book *(The First Five Thousand)*, based on the early work at her Birth Control Clinic, Marie tells a story from her Manchester days, told to her by a woman medical student. The student was helping a male doctor in the outpatient department of a hospital one day when a very sickly baby was brought in by its mother. The mother said that no matter what she tried she could not get the baby to put on weight, or get well. Her previous three babies had also been

Above A young girl with a baby in Wigan in 1921 and *opposite* a large slum family in Bethnal Green in 1923. One of Marie Stopes' main concerns was with the poor.

sickly and had all died in infancy. She thought that this was because there was "something wrong" with her husband. If there was, she said, she would have no more children. The doctor assured her that her husband was quite healthy and that she must continue to "do her duty" by him. It was quite clear, the medical student told Marie Stopes, that the baby was syphilitic—which meant that the father was diseased and that any other children the woman had would also be infected and die too. Such a story must have created a very deep impression.

The second factor was Marie's marriage to Ruggles Gates. It must be remembered that Marie married quite late. At that period many unmarried women of her age would have already decided to stay single. From an early age most of her time had been spent working hard, first to pass examinations and then to further her career. Even while she was involved with Fujii they were separated for most of the time. When she married Gates Marie's character and intellect were mature but she was still sexually naive and inexperienced.

These factors were welded together and made fruitful by her independence and power of mind. This can be seen yet again in the way she responded to the bitter blow of the collapse of her marriage. She did not rely on advice from experts: she went to the British Museum and herself studied the scores of legal and medical books. This quality of mind and personality enabled her to analyse her difficulties and to use them for the benefit of others.

Married Love was published on 26th March, 1918. Essentially, it gives a very romantic view of ideal marriage. The style, however, was suitable only for an educated middle class audience and birth control is just mentioned in passing. The book develops the idea of marriage, and sex, as something for husband and wife to share equally. Marie included some findings of her own on the periodic changes in female desire which she put forward as the scientific explanation of the folk myth of "feminine contrariness." Although her descriptions of the physiology of reproduction and sexual intercourse are very generalized and without diagrams, she does mention the clitoris. She approves of the prostitute's encouragement of "charm and mutual gaiety in pleasure" which were often missing in married couples, and in the eighth edition (of May 1920) she added her approval to the prostitute's active participation in the sexual act and her knowledge of

Opposite Margaret Sanger (1883–1966), the American pioneer of birth control, with her sister in a court room in 1916. She was sentenced and put in prison for opening a birth control clinic in Brooklyn, New York.

Below The Roe brothers at Blackpool Aviation Week in October 1909, Alliott Verdon Roe (1877–1958) on the left and Humphrey Verdon Roe (1878–1949) on the right. Together they built up the famous aircraft firm Avro.

sexual subtleties. But, as a whole, the book was very moderate by our standards.

However, the publication of *Married Love* was not easy. The big established publishers would not publish it; and when she did find a small publisher willing to take on the book he was unable to publish it without financial backing which she was unable to supply. Margaret Sanger, the great American pioneer of birth control, whom Marie Stopes first met at this time, was very impressed when she read the manuscript, and offered to try to find an American publisher for it.

Then Marie met Humphrey Verdon Roe, on leave from the Western Front (the First World War was still in progress) and about to return to France to join a squadron of the Royal Flying Corps. Humphrey Roe had, with his brother, founded the famous aircraft firm Avro, and was himself interested in birth control.

He had already offered to endow a birth control clinic at a Manchester hospital but the offer was refused. He was so impressed by the manuscript of *Married Love* that he immediately offered to lend her the £100 needed to publish it. But the author interested him at least as much as the book and, after a courtship lasting several months, partly conducted by letter while he was fighting in France, they were married in May 1918, soon after the publication of *Married Love*.

Humphrey Roe continued to be an active help and support to Marie. He had long supported female emancipation and the need for female fulfilment. He was a generous and warm person, not a leader of the battle himself, but working hard in close support. In marrying him there was no question of Marie giving up her legal name of "Dr. Marie Stopes." This brought an amusing comment from the famous writer George Bernard Shaw who had known Marie since their mothers had met. (All four were active workers for women's rights.)

"Dear Marie Carmichael Stopes Verdon Roe, as the case may be when this reaches you. You virtually refused to marry me (in the event of my becoming disengaged) because it would *bouleverse* the card catalogues of the world. And now—

  Carmichael Stopes
  see Verdon Roe
  Verdon Roe
  see Roe, Verdon
  see Stopes, Carmichael
  see Humphrey Verdon Roe

  Humphrey Verdon Roe
  see Marie Carmichael Stopes

  Marie Carmichael Stopes
  see—oh, d—n!
  Gives me Ganot's *Physics*

"I shall not be in town tomorrow; why should I rush to contemplate the spectacle of a rival's happiness? And that

The wedding in St. Margaret's, Westminster of Marie Stopes and Humphrey Roe in June 1918. They had, in fact, been married in a Registry Office a month before their church wedding.

book I have ordered! I shall now have to wait for a new edition with the latest revisions. The ceremony *cannot* be of the simplest nature. Do you suppose the Bishop can improvise it to suit the occasion? Oh, you scientific heathens! Well, be happy; and thank you heartily for remembering me,

ever G. Bernard Shaw.''

George Bernard Shaw (1856–1950), who remained a firm friend of Marie (though they did have some differences of opinion) for well over thirty years.

The book was an instant success. It sold 2,000 copies in the first fortnight. Soon a steady stream of letters came in from all over the country asking for birth control advice. Marie quickly sat down to write another book. *Wise Parenthood* was published on 18th November, 1918. It was a slim book, again mainly for a middle class readership, and the first third of it is a summary of *Married Love*. The other twenty or so pages describe ways and means of contraception and there is a sectional diagram of the vagina, cervix and womb, with a cervical cap in position. The recommended technique is a cap with a quinine pessary. The sheath, *coitus interruptus*, "various instruments, some of metal," douching and "safe period" are all discussed but not recommended.

Above The Mothers' Clinic for Constructive Birth Control in its offices in Whitfield Street, where it moved in 1925 from Holloway, and where the Marie Stopes Memorial Centre is now.

Inevitably, Marie now turned her attention to the needs of the working class. How much this was forced on her by the emergence of a specifically working class demand, and how much was due to the influence of Humphrey Roe, who was certainly very conscious of this need, is difficult to say. Either way, it rapidly became a major concern. She published her *Letter to Working Mothers* in April 1919. Although there are occasional lapses into middle-class style, the language is, by and large, simple and direct. After an initial warning against abortion—unsafe and often fraudulent in those days—it gives sound, clear advice on how to obtain and fit a cap. The reader is warned that she may have to try several chemists before she can buy a cap, and is told that if she has any serious difficulty she may write to the author for advice.

In March 1921 Marie and Humphrey Roe opened the Mothers' Clinic in Holloway, London, the first birth control clinic in the country. Several influential people, including the author Arnold Bennett, were persuaded to become patrons. Holloway was a poor district and the Clinic was small and unpretentious. Advice was given free, and the contraceptive methods recommended were cheap so that the poor, whose need was greatest, could afford them. In 1925 the Clinic moved to 108, Whitfield Street, in a poor region behind London's West End, and there it still operates.

Birth control was now becoming Marie Stopes's major concern. As a result her name became known in the country at large, and her work began to receive support from some very influential people. Her main supporters were social reformers, but there were also some progressive and influential doctors and churchmen. She was here attacking a basic social problem. But at the same time she was, without fully realizing it, contributing to one of the major social changes of our century—the move towards permissiveness.

Concentration on birth control led to wide differences of opinion. The first edition of *Married Love* contained a letter from a Jesuit priest. In it he made clear the opposition of the Roman Catholic Church to birth control. But he was able to support her views on marital relations. This letter was deleted from the seventh edition, which came out in May 1919, just fifteen months later. The supporters of the traditional morality settled down to rejecting all aspects of sexual reform as immoral. They determined to drown all Marie's work in the mire of social unacceptability.

In an effort to counter this hardening opposition, Marie asked David Lloyd George, then Prime Minister, for his support. He replied that he could not give it, as so many people thought birth control was a disgrace. But he advised her to hold a great public meeting, to start to make the subject respectable. Never one for doing things by halves, she decided to hold a meeting in the Queen's Hall in London which could seat over 2,000 people, and to organize a platform of speakers from all walks of life. If only a few hundred people had turned up the size of the hall would have made the meeting an obvious failure. But by the time the speakers walked onto the platform, on 31st May, 1921, every seat was filled and many people had to stand. The meeting was a huge success and led to the founding of the Society for Constructive Birth Control and Racial Progress, of which she became president. This society was to provide a firm basis for her work.

Meanwhile, the sales of *Married Love* had topped one hundred thousand copies.

5 Battles and Propaganda

Marie Stopes might have been forgiven for imagining that the biggest battles had been won. After all, the Queen's Hall meeting had shown how many influential supporters she had; and her Society for Constructive Birth Control had the makings of a strong pressure group to finish her work of popular education.

Yet storm clouds were gathering. Opposition to birth control, and to Marie Stopes as its leading exponent, was centred around the Churches and the medical profession (although neither were unanimous in their condemnation). This opposition had the support of many who called themselves "decent clean-minded people." The Roman Catholic Church was quite clear on the matter: contraception other than use of the "safe period" killed sperm, and this was tantamount to murder. A general belief among the churches was that to separate sex from its "natural function" of procreation was sinful. The "decent, clean-

Below Marie and Humphrey on holiday in Switzerland in 1921

minded people" saw birth control as an evil canker in society, which encouraged lust, lured young girls to prostitution and undermined trade and the empire. They feared that if the working classes used birth control their numbers would drop rapidly and ruin the national economy. All these various phrases were used over and over again by opponents of contraception.

The success of the Queen's Hall meeting seemed to make the clouds gather more rapidly than ever. The first rumble of thunder came some five weeks later at a meeting of the Medico-Legal Society in London. Here Anne McIlroy, Professor of Obstetrics and Gynaecology at a London hospital, claimed that the rubber cap of the type recommended by Marie Stopes at her clinic was the most harmful of all methods. At this meeting was Halliday Sutherland, a Roman Catholic doctor. Professor McIlroy's remark gave Dr. Sutherland the idea of writing a book attacking the birth control movement and Marie Stopes personally. The book was called *Birth Control: A Statement of Christian Doctrine against the Neo-Malthusians* and was published in 1922. In it he accused Dr. Stopes of making experiments on the poor, and of using their ignorance to foist birth control on them against their better judgment:

"The ordinary decent instincts of the poor are against these practices, and indeed they have used them less than any other class. But, owing to their poverty, lack of learning, and helplessness, the poor are the natural victims of those who seek to make experiments on their fellows. In the midst of a London slum a woman, who is a doctor of German philosophy (Munich), has opened a Birth Control Clinic, where working women are instructed in a method of contraception described by Professor McIlroy as 'the most harmful method of which I have had experience'. . .It is truly amazing that this monstrous campaign of birth control should be tolerated by the Home Secretary. Charles Bradlaugh was condemned to jail for a less serious crime."

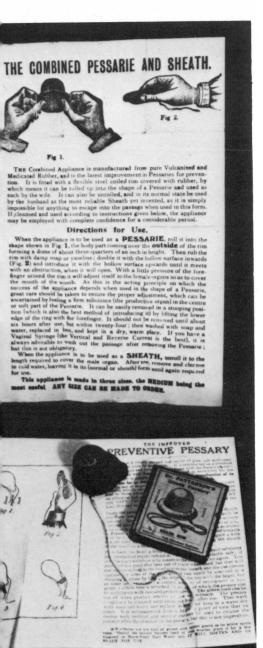

THE COMBINED PESSARIE AND SHEATH.

Fig 1.

Fig 2.

The Combined Appliance is manufactured from pure Vulcanised and Medicated Rubber, and is the latest improvement in Pessaries for prevention. It is fitted with a flexible steel coiled rim covered with rubber, by which means it can be rolled up into the shape of a Pessarie and used as such by the wife. It can also be unrolled, and in its normal state be used by the husband as the most reliable Sheath yet invented, as it is simply impossible for anything to escape into the passage when used in this form. If cleansed and used according to instructions given below, the appliance may be employed with complete confidence for a considerable period.

Directions for Use.

When the appliance is to be used as a **PESSARIE**, roll it into the shape shown in Fig. 1, the body part coming over the **outside** of the rim forming a dome of about three-quarters of an inch in height. Then rub the rim with damp soap or vaseline ; double it with the hollow surface inwards (Fig. 2) and introduce it with the hollow surface upwards until it meets with an obstruction, when it will open. With a little pressure of the fore-finger around the rim it will adjust itself to the female organs so as to cover the mouth of the womb. As this is the acting principle on which the success of the appliance depends when used in the shape of a Pessarie, great care should be taken to ensure the proper adjustment, which can be ascertained by feeling a firm substance (the productive organ) in the centre or soft part of the Pessarie. It can be easily removed in a stooping position (which is also the best method of introducing it) by lifting the lower edge of the ring with the forefinger. It should not be removed until about six hours after use, but within twenty-four ; then washed with soap and water, replaced in box, and kept in a dry, warm place. If you have a Vaginal Syringe (the Vertical and Reverse Current is the best), it is always advisable to wash out the passage after removing the Pessarie ; but this is not obligatory.

When the appliance is to be used as a **SHEATH**, unroll it to the length required to cover the male organ. After use, remove and cleanse in cold water, leaving it in its (normal or sheath) form until again required for use.

This appliance is made in three sizes, the **MEDIUM** being the most useful. **ANY SIZE CAN BE MADE TO ORDER.**

THE IMPROVED PREVENTIVE PESSARY

Above Top Instruction sheet for a combined pessary (early form of cap) and sheath. *Bottom* A check pessary of the type condemned by Professor Anne McIlroy and approved by Marie Stopes.

Marie Stopes realized that this was only the beginning. Unless she did something to stop it, she would be persecuted by people like Dr. Sutherland for the rest of her life. So she brought a suit for libel against him.

The case was heard almost a year later in the High Court before Lord Chief Justice Hewart. It lasted for nine days. Each side had an army of expert witnesses from the medical profession. The chief witness for the defence (Dr. Sutherland and his publishers) was, of course, Professor McIlroy, whose condemnation of the rubber cap had sparked off the whole affair. Appearing in support of Dr. Stopes were such famous men as Sir James Barr, Vice-President of the Medical Association.

As often happens in such cases, the expert evidence was largely contradictory. However, one major fact did emerge which might have had a greater effect on the outcome if everyone's emotions had not been so strong. (Later commentators have even suggested that Lord Hewart himself was biased against Dr. Stopes.) The point was made by Sir Patrick Hastings, K.C., the famous barrister representing Marie Stopes, while cross-examining Professor McIlroy. They were discussing the check pessary which Professor McIlroy had condemned. "Have you ever," asked Hastings, "had a case of a woman who has worn one of these pessaries?"

MCILROY: I have never met a woman yet who was able to fit on the pessary.

HASTINGS: I wonder whether you could answer my question : Have you ever met a case yet of any woman who has worn one?

MCILROY: No.

HASTINGS: So that all you have been telling us at some length in answer to Mr. Charles about the dangers of this is based upon practical experience which does not include one single case of its having been worn?

McILROY: My remarks have been based on experience of occlusion of the womb.

HASTINGS: Quite; but was my question accurate, that it is all based upon experience which does not include one single case where it has been worn?

McILROY: It is not necessary to have a single case.

HASTINGS: The answer is that my question was accurately framed and the answer would be yes?

McILROY: It is not necessary to have a single case.

HASTINGS: When I say it would be yes, perhaps I may say it should be yes?

McILROY: I do not know.

HASTINGS: I do not think that I will trouble you any more about that.

Lord Hewart, however, did not let the matter rest there.

LORD HEWART: But I understand the witness to say, Mr. Hastings—I am sure you want to deal with the point of her answer—

HASTINGS: Certainly.

LORD HEWART: I understand her to say: "True, I have never met a woman who wore a check pessary and had an occlusion of the womb from that cause, but I have had a large experience of the occlusion of the womb, and it is upon that experience, not upon my absence of experience of the check pessary, that my evidence is based." Is that what you say?

McILROY: Yes, my Lord.

HASTINGS: I am much obliged to your Lordship. I quite accept that, but that was not, if I may say so with respect, the point of my question. My question was—let me see if I am quite right, Miss McIlroy —that you never had a case of a woman who had worn one of these check pessaries?

McILROY: No

Professor McIlroy's sweeping condemnation of the rubber check pessary, then, was not based on any practical experience whatsoever. This was a damning admission, largely ignored by the judge in his sum-

Left Sir Patrick Hastings (1880–1952), Counsel for the Prosecution in the suit for libel that Marie Stopes brought against Dr. Halliday Sutherland (1882–1960).

ming up. It was, however, not without its funny side, as we shall see from this story told by Dr. Stopes herself in a later book, *Ten Thousand Cases* (1930).

Some time after the trial Marie heard from some of her patients at her clinic that Professor McIlroy was herself fitting that "most harmful of all methods," the rubber check pessary, at her own hospital clinic. At first she refused to believe these reports, putting them down to lack of knowledge on the part of her patients. In any case, how could someone of Anne McIlroy's standing make such a professional about-turn, without publicly admitting the fact. But the reports still came in, and so to find out for herself Dr. Stopes disguised herself as a charwoman and went along to Professor McIlroy's clinic as a patient. After sitting around for some hours in the waiting room, her turn finally came, and she emerged triumphant soon after having been fitted with a cap by the Professor herself!

In his instruction to the jury the Lord Chief Justice had put four questions for them to answer:

(1) were the words complained of defamatory of the plaintiff?

(2) were they true in substance and in fact?

(3) were they fair comment?

(4) damages, if any?

To the first two questions the jury answered "Yes," to the third they answered "No," and to the fourth they said "One hundred pounds." Taken together, these answers show some conflict. It was suggested at the appeal which followed that, having been badly briefed by the judges, the jury did not really understand the questions. However, although the jury had found the words defamatory, and unfair comment, and had awarded Dr. Stopes damages, Lord Hewart decided that the essence of the case lay in their answer to the second question. So he gave judgment in favour of Halliday Sutherland.

Marie Stopes at once lodged an appeal. Com-

Right Marie Stopes leaving the Law Courts during the 1923 libel action

THE NATIONAL COMMITTEE
FOR THE SUTHERLAND-WAREING APPEAL FUND

Chairman :
EDWARD EYRE, K.C.S.G.

Hon. Treasurer :
THE VISCOUNT CAMPDEN, O.B.E.

Hon. Secretary :
W. P. MARA, K.S.G.

Organisations represented on the Committee :

Catholic Confederation,
Catholic Women's League,
Ladies of Charity,
Catholic Association,

Guild of SS. Luke, Cosmas and Damian,
Catholic Guardians' Association,
National Vigilance Association,
Knights of St. Columba.

Room 10,

5, CHANCERY LANE,

LONDON, W.C. 2.
February 14th 1924.

Dear Madam,

As one having the highest regard for true moral principles you will I feel sure, read the enclosed statement with interest and approval.

Briefly it sets out the salient points of the much-discussed "Birth Control Case" when, as you will no doubt recall, a woman writer on Neo-Malthusian topics instituted legal proceedings for alleged libel against a well-known physician and the publisher of his book.

Whatever the ultimate issue of this action may be, it is satisfactory to record that there is wide-spread recognition of the fact that the defendants in this notable case are clearly not fighting for any personal advantage.

At the express wish of the Cardinal Archbishop of Westminster, and with the full concurrence of the Hierarchy, a National Committee has been formed with the object of raising a fund sufficient to relieve the Defendants of the financial burden they have incurred by being forced into this protracted fight.

Believing you will be anxious to identify yourself in a practical manner with this national movement, the Committee most cordially invite your co-operation and has no hesitation in extending this appeal to those of all denomination who desire the welfare and prosperity of this beloved country.

All contributions will be gratefully acknowledged by the Hon. Treasurer whose name and address appears on the reply envelope accompanying this letter.

Assuring you that any assistance rendered will be fully appreciated, and with anticipated thanks,

I am, Sincerely yours,

Edward Eyre

Chairman.

52

menting on the case shortly afterwards, the *Daily News* said: "We cannot pretend to be satisfied at the position in which legal technicalities as interpreted by the Lord Chief Justice leaves the case, and we regard the decision to appeal as one taken in the interest not merely of the plaintiff but of the public generally."

Before the appeal, six months later, a poison pen campaign was mounted against Marie Stopes, and later on also against the three Lords of Appeal who were to hear the case, a fact which was noted by Lord Justice Scrutton in the Court of Appeal. The appeal was upheld and Marie was awarded even higher damages.

Was this the end? Marie asked her solicitor to make informal enquiries of the solicitor to the other side. The answer came back that this was the end. Could she then look forward to security? Could she build, at last, a family life? She was thirty-eight when she married Humphrey Roe. After a year she had given birth to a son but he had died during birth. Four years later, now that the way seemed clear, they decided to try again.

But victory had not been won. There could be no end for the defenders of the traditional morality—no end but final victory for "purity." Eternal souls were (they believed) at stake. The Church of Rome did not fail in its duty (as it saw it) of leadership. The case went to the House of Lords and Dr. Sutherland won. That *was* final. Marie Stopes had lost.

But did she really lose? Certainly the cost to her of fighting the case was enormous: not only did she have to pay back all the damages, she had to pay the defendants' costs as well as her own. The cost to her personal life, too, was very great. The case had gone on for almost two years. It was a time of almost constant work and worry. Rather than leaving everything to her legal advisers, she insisted on working on the details of the case herself. The final stages ran through her pregnancy and the birth of her only living child,

Left A fund-raising letter from the Chairman of the National Committee for the Sutherland-Waring Appeal Fund, Sir Edward Eyre. The Committee was made up of a number of religious organizations who were united in their opposition to Marie Stopes and her views on birth control.

the author of this book. Through all this, the normal work of running the clinic went on, and grew, and she was in great demand as a public speaker.

The biggest gain to her from the trial was all the publicity. Birth control suddenly became a national issue, and clinics began to open all over the country. The sales of *Married Love* also increased dramatically—the copy mentioned by the judge at the first trial in February 1923 (almost exactly five years after publication) belonged to the tenth edition, at which time 191,000 copies had been published. By the end of the following year sales had reached half a million.

This was only the start of a long series of skirmishes with "the opposition" which were to last for a long time. For example, Marie made a film called *Married Love or Maisie's Marriage,* intended to be a general interest film rather than birth control propaganda. Nevertheless, public showings were held up while the Chief Censor, a Roman Catholic, demanded cuts. However, local Watch Committees in many parts of the country allowed it to be shown uncut and it was very popular. Marie was also discriminated against by some newspapers. *The Times,* for example, refused to publish any advertisements for her books. Her play *Vectia,* about the desire of a virgin wife for a child by her husband, was banned by the Lord Chamberlain. It was the subject matter and not any detail that he objected to. Never one to be stopped by such trifling obstacles, she sat down with a special high speed stenographer and wrote a new play from scratch in six hours. It was typed overnight and the script was back at the theatre the next morning. Called *Our Ostriches: A Play of Modern Life,* it ran for three months.

Marie was later involved in two more law suits. One of them resulted directly from her action against Halliday Sutherland, and involved contempt of court by two Roman Catholic newspapers, the *Tablet* and the *Universe,* by publishing comment on the Stopes-

Right The Times, among other newspapers and journals, refused for a time to publish any advertisements for books by Marie Stopes.

Reprints now in Stock

Lucy and the Little Red Horse

Children's Book with Coloured Illustrations

Nora Unwin

7 6

Nursery Rhymes

Illustrated

6 6

Gray's Elegy

Illustrated

Thomas Gray

2 6

George Crabbe

The Library

Illustrated 2/6

Garcia Lorca as a Painter

Illustrated

Gregorio Prieto

7 6

Omar Khayyam: The Rubaiyat

Fitzgerald's First Translation

Illustrated

5/-

Instead of Tears

by

Dr. Marie Stopes

(*Author of Married Love*)

5/-

Decorated edition of this famous elegy, first publication as a book.

De La More Press

Alex. Moring Ltd., 2a, Cork Street, W.1

Reprints now in Stock

Lucy and the Little Red Horse

Children's Book with Coloured Illustrations

Nora Unwin

7/6

Nursery Rhymes

Illustrated

6/6

Gray's Elegy

Illustrated

Thomas Gray

2/6

George Crabbe

The Library

Illustrated 2/6

Garcia Lorca as a Painter

Illustrated

Gregorio Prieto

7/6

Omar Khayyam: The Rubaiyat

Fitzgerald's First Translation

Illustrated

5/-

De La More Press

Alex. Moring Ltd., 2a, Cork Street, W.1

Sutherland case while it was still being heard. In the other case she was herself sued for libel by the editor of the *Morning Post;* she had suggested that the reason they banned an advertisement for her Society for Constructive Birth Control (which had run for six whole years) was the influence of a Roman Catholic plot to muzzle the English press. She lost, and had to pay £200 damages.

In other ways Marie's work was going well. Besides being in great demand as a public speaker in most of the provincial cities, she was invited to lecture at the more progressive medical schools.

Below Humphrey, Marie and their young son, Harry (the author of this book) in May 1930.

6 *The Needs of the Poor*

In December 1929 *Mother England* was published, a collection of letters received by Dr. Stopes from women (and some men) from all over the country and as far away as Canada. Many of the writers were poor working class women with little or no education. Their scrawled letters tell a dreadful story of anxiety, ignorance, fear of repeated pregnancies, and guilt at denying their husbands sexual intercourse as a final desperate measure to stop conception.

"Dear Dr. Stopes

I am 32 yrs. old married to a compositor, 10 yrs. and one child aged 5½ yrs.—Through ill attention or bad-management, I was injured when my little one was born (the doctor being partly drunk) and I am unable to carry another child more than 2 or 2½ months, miscarriage *always* happening. The last was just over a year ago, when the doctor told my husband, if I had another it would mean going into hospital with prolapsus, and my womb taken away.

"My husband said at once that must not be and had refrained from any relation whatever since that time, but lately he is beginning to fret under the strain, being the average, strong, healthy working man, and although there is no word of reproach, the fits of irritableness and bad temper, are getting worse and more often, and I feel sure will end in a separation soon if nothing can be done. I have a lot of Spanish blood too in my veins which doesn't help any, living as we have to do and is wearing my nerves to pieces. Will you *please* tell me what I could do or get to use to prevent being pregnant, (as the doctors say I'll never be able to carry another child the full time—but refused to tell me what I was to do—If you will help me, you will make our home happy and peaceful once more, and I will be so truly grateful.

Yours respectfully
N.-E.-C.

"Our house is only a lodge belonging to the 'big house' so will you please put Lodge in case the lady might see it and not approve of my trying to prevent being pregnant, as the rich seem to think a working woman has no right to know anything, at least that has been my own experience."

"Dear Dr. Stopes,
I have one little boy 5 years old, and would not have minded another but I am terrified, for I have had two miscarriages through nothing but weakness followed by Pneumonia; My Doctor even thought I would have to go in a Sanitorium, and the thoughts of being pregnant again is really awful. So would you be so kind as to give me your advice, for I have a real good Husband who has studied my health for the last 10 months; but I often wonder is it fair to him.

Yours Truly
M.–H."

Below Letters arrived for Marie Stopes from all over the world, many, like this one from Copenhagen, with no more than her name and a guess at where she lived for an address.

And there were many other letters like these.

Of the women who actually visited her clinic, over ninety-nine per cent claimed to be married. The rest were mainly young couples who said they were engaged, and sought advice for example about whether existing disease would threaten the girl's life if she became pregnant. Only five women out of the total on whom Dr. Stopes reported in her book *Ten Thousand Cases* were unmarried mothers. Commenting on this she said, "we see nothing of the 'frivolous type' which opponents say patronize birth control clinics." Twenty-seven per cent had already used birth control methods before.

Some insight into the condition of the women who came to the clinic for help is given in the table which is adapted from *Ten Thousand Cases:*

Maternal histories of mothers whose pregnancies occurred before attending the clinic						
Pregnancies				Disasters		
No. of times pregnant	Cases	Total pregnancies	Live children (per cent)*	Deaths after birth (per cent)*	Miscarriages (per cent)*	Total (per cent)*
1 time	1,950	1,950	91	5	7	12
2 times	2,094	4,188	90	5	7	12
3 times	1,554	4,662	85	5	7	12
4 times	998	3,992	79	7	14	21
5 times	597	2,985	76	8	16	24
6 times	362	2,172	75	9	15	25
7 times	245	1,715	73	10	17	27
8 times	164	1,312	72	12	17	29
9 times	100	900	71	11	17	29
10 times	64	640	70	14	17	31
11 times	45	495	69	14	16	31
12 times	38	456	61	19	20	39
13 times	15	195	60	22	18	40

*These figures are expressed as percentages of the total number of pregnancies.

These figures must not be taken as representative of the whole population, and precise deductions cannot be drawn from them. Yet we can take them as broadly representative of working class, or lower working class, conditions at that time. The trends are quite clear. The more times a woman becomes pregnant the greater are her chances of having a miscarriage and the more likely is a child born to her to die in early infancy. In fact, for women having one or two pregnancies, nine out or ten of these pregnancies will result in live births which survive infancy; while the woman who has had thirteen (on average) at least five of them either miscarry or die soon after birth.

Commenting on these figures, Dr. Stopes herself said, "One point of special interest which emerges is that the ordinary statistical birth and infant death rates are very misleading as indices of the toll of motherhood and that a woman's contribution to motherhood is represented more truly by our clinical statistics, for the strain upon a woman's physique of a natural miscarriage or a criminal abortion has to be reckoned into the total physiological strain of her motherhood. When we are considering motherhood naturally the question of the numbers of the deaths *in utero* is not to be ignored in considering the worth of our national resources, both physiological and economic."

Right A nurse at the Mothers' Clinic in London talking to a patient.

Below A cheque for the Mothers' Clinic from Edward, Duke of Windsor.

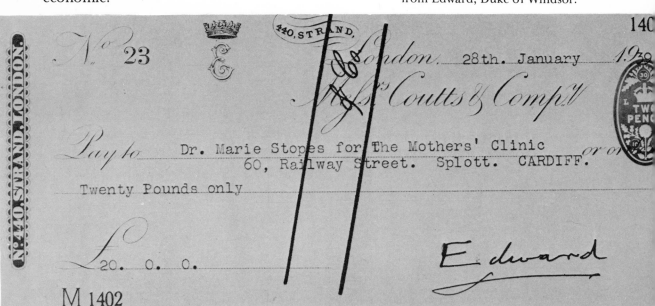

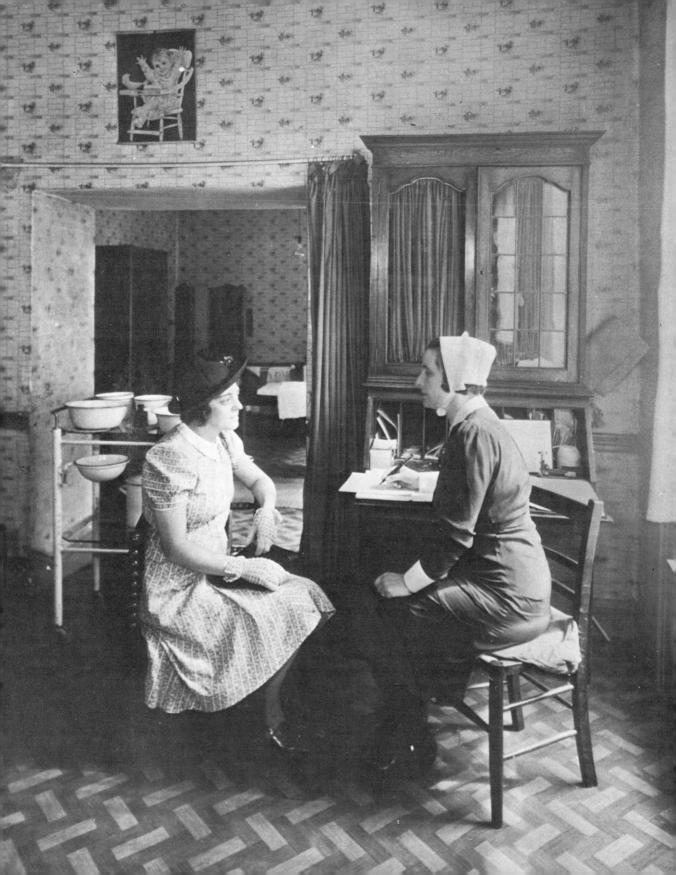

The deliberately low keyed, sympathetic atmosphere at the Mother's Clinic helped timid women to talk about themselves and to tell things that they would probably have hidden from the doctors at a hospital clinic. In this way Marie Stopes was able to build up a mine of information which was not available from other sources on such questions as the use of abortion as a means of birth control.

The staffing of the clinic by midwives rather than qualified doctors (although there were two women doctors who could be called upon as visiting specialists) encouraged the informal atmosphere and had other practical advantages. The most important was that it could have longer opening hours than would otherwise have been possible: from its beginning the clinic stayed open from 10 a.m. until 6 p.m. on three days a week and from 5.00 p.m. until 8 p.m. on the other two days.

At the outset some women came to the clinic who had never had any children and, for various reasons, did not want a family. As pressure on the clinic mounted, however, it was decided that only those who had a family, the size of which they wanted to limit, could be seen. By 1924, 5,000 cases had been dealt with. By 1930 Marie Stopes was writing: "The years which have passed. . .have led to a great improvement in the literature available, and a number of Clinics have been founded to carry on the work all over the country, so that almost saturation point has been reached in connection with the normal and healthy. Those now coming to the Clinic are largely and will increasingly be the difficult cases—those suffering from some disability in body which makes it difficult satisfactorily to use the information in books."

An aspect of her work which was and is often forgotten was the work done by her clinic to help people *have* children. This attempt to help childless couples wanting children was a vital part of the Clinic's activity from its foundation. Her maxim was

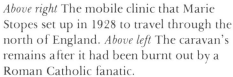

Above right The mobile clinic that Marie Stopes set up in 1928 to travel through the north of England. *Above left* The caravan's remains after it had been burnt out by a Roman Catholic fanatic.

"Babies in the right place." It was an ingredient of the name "Constructive Birth Control." A number of women who came for this "pro-conceptive" advice had already had several miscarriages. But, curiously, several others married for up to nine years were found to be virgins and quite ignorant of the fact that sex was needed to have a baby!

The demand for advice was great. By 1924, in addition to the 5,000 cases treated by the Clinic, a further 30,000 had either written or come to the Clinic for literature. It was a time of great activity in the birth control movement as a whole. Dr. Stopes provided a caravan set up as a mobile clinic in 1928 to travel through the north of England, but in the following year it was burned to the ground by a Roman Catholic fanatic.

Meanwhile her London clinic was busy training doctors and nurses in the methods of birth control. The midwife in charge of the first official hospital clinic, opened in 1925, was trained there. However, the job of opening clinics in the provinces was mainly left to the Malthusian Society for the Provision of Birth Control Clinics. Their first two were in Walworth and North Kensington in London. The first provincial clinic was opened in Wolverhampton in 1925 and this developed an offshoot in Cannock Chase for miners' wives. Soon every major city in the country had its own clinic.

The impact on the Government, however, was slow. In 1922, a health visitor with the Edmonton District Council's public health department began to give birth control advice. For this she was sacked. Over the next few years there was mounting pressure from all kinds of organizations and individuals for Government recognition of the need to provide birth control advice. A group prominent in this work was the Women's Co-Operative Guild. Not until 1930 did the first crack appear in the Government's defences. This was a secret memorandum saying that "where there are *medical grounds* for giving advice on contraception methods to married women in attendance at the [child welfare] Centres, it may be given but. . .such advice should be limited to *cases where further pregnancy would be detrimental to health,* and should be given at a separate session." The concession in this memorandum is small, but it is there, and it was up to interested organizations to enlarge it by applying pressure in the right way. The first push was given by Marie Stopes who somehow got hold of a copy and published it in her journal *Birth Control News.*

Reaction to the growing success of the birth control movement was varied. Under the headline "The Comparative Danger to the State of Moral Defectives and Mental Defectives" the *Catholic Herald* made a violent attack on the supporters of birth control in general

OCHONE
OCHONE

TINK AV THE
DISGRACE TO
OULD OIRELAND

'TIS THE CINSOR,
BEDAD!

WHIROO!
IHE
PRISICINT
HIMSILF.

H, TIS A TIRRIBLE TING
FOR THE WOIFE WID HER
TIN BRATS AND ALL
AND ALL. BAD CESS TO THE
DIRTY SHPALPEEN

ATTEMPTED REVOLUTION IN DUBLIN.

CAPTURE OF DESPERATE PERSON FOUND TO BE IN
POSSESSION OF COMPLETE SET OF MARIE STOPES.

LOW'S ALMANACK.

PROPHECIES FOR *1931*

Above The famous cartoon by David Low which made fun of the Irish Catholic Church's attitude towards Marie Stopes and her writings.

and Marie Stopes in particular. It accused them of demanding "The sterilization of the unfit" which was, of course, quite untrue. The article went on, "One, Marie Stopes, with her destructive propaganda is a more terrible foe to morality, liberty, progress and all for which Christianity stands, than ten thousand mental deficients." This was in August 1930. Another reaction may be seen in a contemporary cartoon by Low, which appeared later in the same year.

Marie Stopes reacted characteristically to these attacks by the Roman Catholic Church. She made a defiant and flamboyant gesture. She published a book on *Roman Catholic Methods of Birth Control;* and she took a copy into the Catholic cathedral at Westminster, and fastened it to the font with a chain and padlock. She then threw away the key. But she took care to tell the Press first, as her plan was to attract publicity even at the risk of being caught in the act.

Marie Stopes and Humphrey Verdon Roe in the garden of their home, Givons Grove, at Leatherhead, Surrey, in the early 1920s.

7 The Last Years

The final phase of Marie Stopes's life began, by her own reckoning, in the "early summer of 1938." In the following year she published the first of a series of volumes of poetry, *Love Songs for Young Lovers*. In a note contained in that book she says that the period of twenty years which she had vowed to devote to social service had ended in 1938 and that, as a result, she felt freer to devote herself to poetry. The break, however, was not a clean one but rather a slow unwinding from her intense activities of the early 1930s.

From the publication of *Married Love* Marie Stopes had been the major propagandist, thinker, and controversialist of the birth control movement. There were, however, other workers and organizations active in this field and, as we saw in chapter 6, they too founded clinics. There was a great deal of co-operation between the various bodies, as well as overlapping of vice-presidents and members of their councils. Some form of unification was clearly inevitable as well as desirable. The first step was taken in 1930 when Marie Stopes suggested a body to co-ordinate the work of the various birth control organizations. This was set up under the presidency of Lord Horder with herself on the governing body. It was named the National Birth Control Council, Later renamed the National Birth Control Association.

But the unity of 1930 did not last long. Marie Stopes was not an easy person to work with, and this unity was itself an attempt to patch over previous disruptions. Her tendency to bulldoze the opposition into the ground, her inability to tolerate contradiction or other points of view, her insistence that everyone should acknowledge her leadership and pioneering work—all this made her a powerful public speaker, but it also made the whole idea of co-operation difficult. Nevertheless, she was capable of great sweetness and charm, particularly when she felt that her ideals and views were not threatened.

As she grew older she hardened in her ways so that her position inside the movement became more and more isolated, moving towards that of figurehead and scapegoat. In 1933 she resigned from the National Birth Control Association, splitting the Society for Constructive Birth Control from it. The pioneering work of the Society for Constructive Birth Control had been done. The N.B.C.A. (renamed the Family Planning Association in 1939) expanded, and they provided a network of clinics throughout the country.

In her early days in Manchester Professor Alexander, the philosopher, had predicted that one day Marie would turn to poetry. Her first collection, *Man, Other Poems and a Preface,* was published in 1914. Her own plan "to spend twenty years on scientific research, then twenty years on philosophy, and then twenty years in the direct service of humanity, meanwhile writing one poem in which to embody a life's experience of the universe, and when the poem was finished—to die!," which was described in the preface, was not quite fulfilled. But poetry was what she valued most in the end.

Reaction to her poetry was mixed. After the publication of *Love Songs for Young Lovers* (1939), George Bernard Shaw wrote to her: "Your scientific background is interesting, as it produces an impersonality that is new in love poems and gives them an unusual dignity. You are a poet all right. It can't be helped." *Out of the Noise,* two stanzas of which are quoted below, was highly praised by Lord Alfred Douglas:

Out of the noise
Out of the noisome fumes
Out of the fuming funnel of the City

Above Marie and Humphrey with Keith Briant (1913–) on the left and Lord Alfred Douglas (1870–1945) on the right.

Crept like a wisp of pity
A gliding shape.

Then suddenly like day
Breaking the dawn in May
Up to the light
Up to the lightsome joy
Up to the joyous radiance of day
Flashed sight, on wings away
Leaping with joyance swift through vibrant space,
Love's grace.

Lord Alfred Douglas—notorious because of his close friendship with Oscar Wilde—was to become her last great "cause." This strange relationship began when she wrote to him asking how to get her poetry published, and it went on for some time by letter. She at last managed to meet him, with a piece of subterfuge. A devout Roman Catholic, Lord Alfred was heartily opposed to anything to do with birth control. This fact must have been uppermost in Marie Stopes's mind, since she signed all of her letters to him "Marie Carmichael." Not until the meeting was fixed did she reveal who she was. Lord Alfred was astounded when in February 1939 he received a letter from Marie signed "Marie Stoops." "As a Catholic," he wrote back, "I disagree with your view on birth control." But their friendship ripened.

Marie Stopes admired Douglas as a poet despite his religious views. He was the greatest writer of sonnets living, and this form she considered supreme. Douglas was at this time living in rather genteel poverty and finding it very hard to make ends meet. As the relationship developed, Marie Stopes spent much of her time trying to get him a State pension. She bullied and cajoled everyone she could think of who might carry influence in this direction, wrote scores of letters, and organized petitions to the Prime Minister. But in the end it was to no avail; the pension was never awarded.

A Primrose

A primrose moss enwarded upwards peers
Into celestial whorls with a calm eye
Straight into swift revolving heavenly sphe[res]
Nor quivers at immensities on high.

Its golden circlet, calmly star-like planne[d]
To show no sign of all the inner surge
Of von hordes, atomic conflicts fanned
To feed with revolutions swift life's urge
Its stilly lucent surface symmetry
Pleases my eye, reflects within my hear[t]
A pool of peace chear cut from strife. May I
Thus hold a radiant pattern on my part
Daring serenely from my clamorous sod
To be myself, and please the eye of God.

70

The scientist as poet brought science into her poetry, as in *The Primrose*:

A primrose, moss encircled, upward peers
Into celestial whorls, with a calm eye
Straight into swift revolving spheres,
Nor quivers at immensities on high.
Its golden circlet, calmly star-like planned
To show no sign of all the inner surge
Of ion hordes, atomic conflicts fanned
To feed with revolutions life's swift urge.
Its stilly, lucent, surface symmetry
Pleases my eye, reflects within my heart
A pool of peace clear cut from strife. May I
Thus hold a radiant pattern on my part
Daring serenely from my clamorous sod
To be myself, and please the eye of God.

The Poet Laureate, John Masefield, another admirer of her work, wrote: "I hope you will write more poems like *We Burn*. In these you are doing well what no one else could do." "What no one else could do" was to fuse science and poetry without distorting the one, or cheapening the other. The underlying theme of *We Burn* is the production of energy in all living things by the oxygenation of carbon atoms—burning:

We speak of fire
When Oxygen leaps swift
In fierce embrace to carbon,
Then the lift
Of heat flicks red-hot tongues
So fierce they heavenward aspire.
Eyes that perceive the smoke,
The glow, the cinder,
Of swift embrace divalent,
Yet are blind
When the same force plays on a lower scale
Whose ranges lend to man his lissom life
His power, his love, and all his leaping strife.

Left The original manuscript of Marie Stopes' poem *The Primrose*.

. . . . .
Cool Truth proclaims
Life lives by burning.
Tuned to our slow-scaled speed in ceaseless fire we dwell
Breathing a smoke so cool
We in the plangent rhythm of life's heart
Know not the pain of burning, but apart
Live, love, serenely in each rose-flecked cell.

But even at this stage of her life when she was no longer so concerned with the birth control movement, she was still the victim of acts of petty persecution for the part she had played in it. In her *Evidence to the Royal Commission on the Press* she quotes many instances of discrimination against her by newspapers, who either refused to publish her advertisements, or deleted references to her earlier books (e.g. *Married Love*) from them.

In 1932 Humphrey and Marie and their son Harry moved into the house that was to be Marie's final home. This house she looked on as her real "home," unlike all the other houses in which she had lived. It gave her peace and contentment, solitude and freedom. It gave her wonderful views and a sense of graciousness and space. These things were vital to her, even in the later years of her life, when she was living almost alone, and when the burden of keeping up a large place was almost too much for her.

This house, Norbury Park, set in the middle of beechwoods in the Surrey hills, is a beautifully proportioned Georgian mansion, full of light and dignity. In the 1930s, before the Second World War, it was the setting for a great deal of entertaining; many well-known literary and scientific people came there as Marie's guests. During these years, the house was run with the minimum of staff, and with Marie always firmly in charge of all the details.

When war began in 1939, Humphrey Roe went off to join the R.A.F. (although he and Marie had, in fact, led largely separate lives for some years) and the staff

Right Norbury Park where Marie, Humphrey and Harry moved in 1932.

were dispersed. She still did a lot of entertaining, but on a smaller and simpler scale, even when her domestic help was reduced to two. Fortunately she had always enjoyed cooking; and she had strong opinions about a healthy diet, which were reflected in her recipes and menus.

Marie had always managed the clinics herself, and a part of the spacious basement of Norbury Park was used for clinic business and all the postal business was moved there early in the war. She attended to this herself daily until her final illness, supervising a number of secretaries who worked on her voluminous correspondence. Thus, the otherwise quiet house had some activity still below stair, even to the end.

But above stairs, as the 1950s drew on, her life grew lonelier and more withdrawn. Humphrey died in 1949; her son married, much against her will, in 1948. Although she was always glad to see her grandchildren, she and her son and daughter-in-law were never really reconciled.

Marie had been moulded by her battles and the opposition she had met; she could only have survived, and done what she did by having a very tough nature in addition to being romantic and idealistic. In her later years, her fighting spirit turned to bitterness and she became estranged from many of her former admirers and supporters. Her personal secretary, Mrs. Windley, who now runs the Stopes Memorial Clinic, continued to work with her throughout these difficult years and cared for her at the end.

Apart from this support and that of a few warm friends, Marie lived in solitude. The only two human residents of this beautiful and once lively house were now herself, ageing and embittered, and the old servant who had come from a mental home. The third inhabitant was Marie's beloved dog, a chow, who had been her faithful companion for twelve years.

She died on 2nd October, 1958, thirteen days

Left The London Mothers' Clinic after bomb damage during the Second World War.

before her seventy-eighth birthday. She had been ill for more than a year, but had fought her battle privately and alone, and continued to work and live as if nothing were wrong. She refused normal medical attention, and was unwilling to show weakness to anyone. So she remained in her beloved house, and there she died.

Below Marie and Cherry, her black chow, in 1952 at Norbury Park.

8 *Epitaph*

The Times, in its obituary, said of her, "Dr. Marie Stopes can fairly be said to have transformed the thoughts of her generation about the physical aspects of marriage and the role of contraception in married life." Another obituary said that she would one day be recognized as one of the most influential figures in the history of British medicine.

Only after her death can we really begin to understand the real significance of Marie Stopes. She has come to be associated with birth control but that was only one aspect of her real concerns. To understand what she has done to society we must return to the problems from which she started, and we must follow through the implications of birth control.

Her book *Married Love* was about personal relations in marriage, not about birth control. It recognized the vital importance of sexual union to the happiness of the partners, and their equality. Both man and woman should understand each other, and both should *enjoy* the relationship. This was the core of her ideas about marriage. The need for birth control was an obvious consequence if one faced the realities of sexual union and family life. Thus *Married Love* included a few pages arguing obliquely for birth control, and half a page of the most sketchy information upon techniques. That was all that was relevant to her book. Her interests in writing it lay elsewhere.

What was so revolutionary in *Married Love*? First, to look upon joyous mutuality as the heart of sexual love; second, to pass from this to biological realities. Her concern with sexual love was restricted to its role in marriage; but her understanding of biological realities included those of birth control. Her breaching of traditional morality really was extremely small, but the fact that she made such a breach at all was highly significant.

Circumstances forced attention on to birth control. There, morality came face to face with practical problems. And both were highly charged emotionally. Marie Stopes wrote on page 89 of the first edition of *Married Love* of how twelve children "sap a woman's vitality, so little strength has she that nearly 60 per cent of these later ones die." Father St. John, the Jesuit priest, whose letter was published in the early editions, answered the point in this letter in terms of "Eternity...The Catholic belief is that the loss of health on her part for a few years of life and the diminished vitality on the part of her later children would be a very small price to pay for an endless happiness on the part of all." It was the suffering poor women who really won the day.

Marie Stopes had not wanted to get too involved in birth control—but everyone else either held traditional views or feared to act against them. At last she and Humphrey Roe said, "We seem to be the only two people independent enough, and with the necessary freedom, resources and determination, to do it. No one can stop us, and obviously we have got to do it ourselves." Looking back, we should acknowledge their bravery and personal devotion.

Thanks to the battles of fifty years ago, we have the right to know the ways in which we can control our own lives with respect to childbearing. We still do not have complete and genuine freedom of access to information and supplies, but the principle is established and the details are coming. We now have the problem of what to do with our freedom. We must go back and solve the moral problems.

What of the work of the Stopes Memorial Centre today? It provides a normal birth control service such as is now available throughout the country, largely through the Family Planning Association. A vital extension of this, the Domiciliary Service, was also

Above Harry Stopes-Roe and family with Sir Russell (now Lord) Brain at the opening of the Marie Stopes Memorial Clinic in Whitefield Street, London on 12th May, 1961.

built up alongside the F.P.A. Thousands of women are so ground down with poverty, often complicated by subnormality, that they are unable to go to a clinic for help. Do we not have the right—the duty—to take help to those who need it, but are unable to come to us? Yet continuing opposition to birth control means that even now, effective measures are still thwarted. Some health visitors help; many do not. The integration of birth control with maternal and child care services is yet to come.

In 1963 the Stopes Centre started the Young People's Advisory Centre. The words "Young People" refer in fact to unmarried people and this was the problem. The F.P.A. had not been able to approach this area of activity. Its middle-class supporters would not have stood for it. Interestingly enough, despite the title of the service, the age of those attending ranged up to forty-five. It was the only service prepared openly to advise the unmarried. Quite soon after its inception, it was decided to set an upper age of twenty-three, and the main Stopes Centre agreed to see the older ones. Within two years the demand from young people was so great that the first Brook Advisory Centre was set up, followed by many others all over the country; and now the F.P.A. itself is prepared to advise "unmarrieds."

Our forefathers had rationalized their attitudes towards sex in terms of Divine Law, in terms of a supposed supernatural "Nature" to the sexual act, and in terms of supposed dire medical consequence. Naturally, those in authority in the religious and the medical spheres came to believe their statements to be true. Now many of these beliefs are questioned. If we abandon "God's Word" and the "medical facts" what rules, if any, should govern our sexual behaviour?

We can only solve this problem by thinking hard about the foundations of morality, together with practical work exploring the realities of moral experience. The services provided by the Stopes Memorial Centre (of which a few have been mentioned here) are doing today what is called for today, just as Marie Stopes herself did what was called for fifty years ago. The interesting thing is that Marie Stopes would, if she were alive, surely disapprove of what is being done now. This, I think, shows something of the nature of real pioneering. Marie Stopes had extreme clarity, foresight and courage; but she was moulded by her age, not by the age that she brought into being. She could not herself be "post-Stopesian" in her outlook. She set in motion something even greater than she herself could have imagined.

Appendix: Birth Control Then and Now

Birth control has been practised from ancient times though scientific discussion and practice are quite recent. The term "birth control" itself was first used in print by Margaret Sanger, the American expert, in 1914. Curiously the term "contraception" goes back nearly fifty years earlier. The two terms are often confused, but "birth control" is really the wider and includes any method of controlling birth. The idea of "control" is fundamental to both. The purpose of contraception is to allow intercourse without leading to children.

Below Margaret Sanger (*front row, right*), the American pioneer of birth control, as a student nurse.

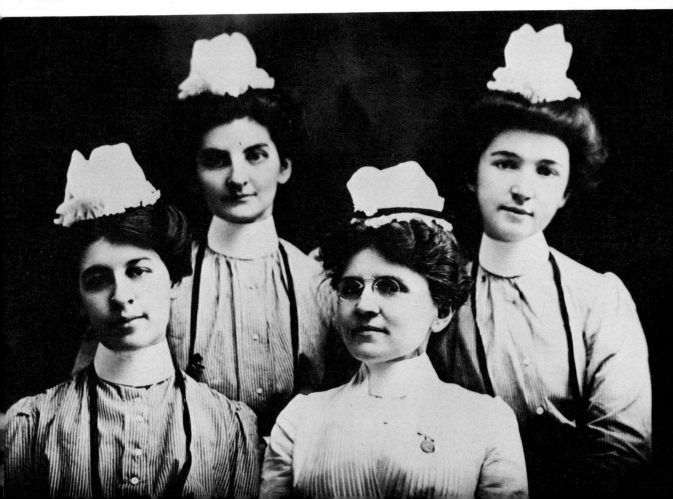

It may be achieved in three ways:
a) by acting on the man and/or his sperm,
b) by acting on the woman and/or her ova,
c) by placing some mechanical or chemical barrier between the two.

So far, direct action on the man has not been successful. *Vasectomy* is entirely satisfactory for those who will never again want to have children, but most surgeons would tell you that it is irreversible and ends the possibility of conception. In the rare and unlikely event of a man regretting the operation some surgeons will consider doing another operation and, when well done, the chances of a return to fertility may reach fifty per cent, but no man should undergo vasectomy unless he is certain that he can accept it as final. The vasectomy operation itself is very simple and does not in any physical way stop either the man or the woman from enjoying sex to the full.

It is surprising that contraception via the woman has proved technically more possible than via the man. In fact, direct action upon the woman is now the most popular method of contraception in the form of the Pill

The *Oral Contraceptive* (the Pill as it is known) works by altering the balance of certain chemicals (called hormones) in the woman's body. A state is produced in the body which is sufficiently like pregnancy to stop it producing and caring for ova. If the Pill is correctly taken, this method may be looked on as 100 per cent effective. Despite the variety of chemical substances available, the method is not perfect. Some of the materials used upset some women, and it seems that a few women are upset by all varieties. Some of the side effects are more serious, but with medical supervision the method is generally acceptable. This contraceptive method, however, though probably the most commonly used today, has become available only within the past twenty years; it is a recent development and not a direct result of the work of Marie Stopes.

Right The Pill in production.

The *Intra Uterine Device* (I.U.D.), which is in our second grouping, is growing in popularity. It has a longer history. Exactly how it works is not entirely clear and for a very few women it does not work at all; a somewhat larger number eject the device or have other complications. When it does work, it works very well, and needs no attention for a whole year. It keeps the womb in such a condition that it will not accept and care for a fertilized ovum. It does not prevent ovulation, and menstruation proceeds normally.

An earlier version of the I.U.D., the *Grafenberg Ring,* was widely used in the 1920s, though Marie Stopes disapproved of this. It was particularly appreciated by the young, for it gave them a sense of freedom. However, the ring went out of favour during the 1930s to be later replaced by the modern I.U.D.

The main methods of contraception used in the 1920s before scientific methods became available and accepted was *Coitus Interruptus*. In this the penis is withdrawn just as the man is about to reach his climax, so that the sperm is spilled outside and does not get inside the woman. This method has the serious

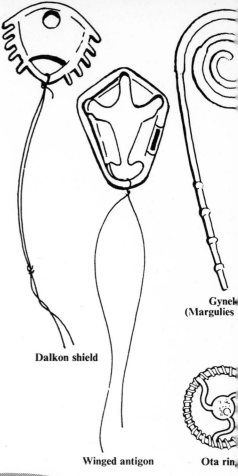

Dalkon shield

Gynek
(Margulies

Winged antigon

Ota rin

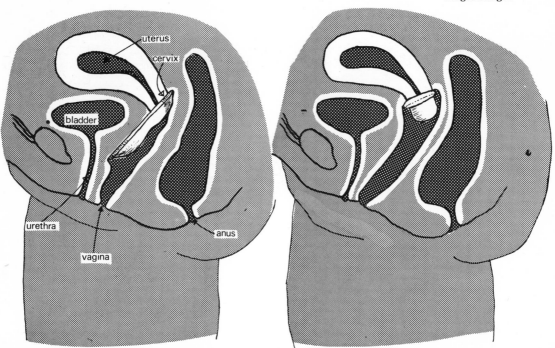

Above left A Dutch cap and *above right* a cervical cap in position.

84

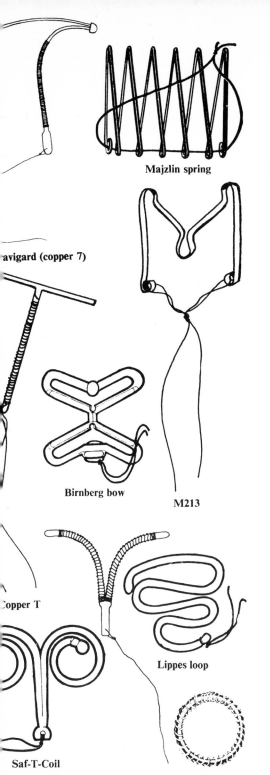

Majzlin spring

Gravigard (copper 7)

Birnberg bow

M213

Copper T

Lippes loop

Saf-T-Coil

Soonawala copper device　**Hall-Stone ring**

Above and opposite above Various I.U.D.s, actual size.

disadvantage of being unnerving and shatters any possibility of mutual fulfillment; it is also very inefficient (63 per cent of the first 5,000 patients at the new Clinic who had used any form of contraception at all had used this method, and it had failed in 82 per cent of these cases).

The next most widely used method in the 1920s was the *Condom* or *Sheath* (it was reported by 15 per cent of the cases, and its failure rate was 75 per cent) and the *Quinine Pessary* (9 per cent of the cases had used it, with a failure rate of 98 per cent). In fairness to these methods, we must note that the failure rates given above were reported by people who wanted a better method than those which they had already tried; many more people who were satisfied by these methods are not included in these figures. Modern condoms are reliable, and modern *chemical spermicides,* of which the quinine pessary was an early example, are fairly efficient.

We now come to the "classic" methods of modern contraception: the various forms of the cap. Only two main kinds will be described here, the *Cervical* cap and

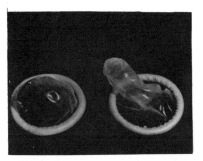

Above Condoms, rolled up, unrolled, and being tested for leaks.

85

Above Family planning posters in Lahore, West Pakistan.

the *diaphragm* (or Dutch Cap). The diagrams make the methods of operation clear. The caps are made of rubber, the diaphragm having a spring-steel ring inside the roll of the tim. The cap in any form is normally used with a spermicidal cream or jelly; it is put into place before intercourse and removed eight hours or so later. Both forms of vaginal cap were known among the rich and privileged from the 1880s, but the cervical cap was first described some forty years earlier. Marie Stopes developed the use of the cervical form in particular because it covered less of the vagina, and because—unlike the diaphragm which lodged in place by pressing against the vaginal walls—it carried no risk of progressively stretching the vagina.

There is another way of placing a barrier to stop the sperm meeting the ovum. It is the simplest and

Above Various caps, soluble pessaries and a sponge of the 1920s.

cheapest of these methods, and is the most useful for the poorest people. Marie Stopes spent much effort in her later life, after the Second World War, in trying to make it available in India. For that country, the method consists simply of a pad of cotton waste soaked in cooking oil, placed at the top of the vagina around the cervix. Both ingredients are readily available in India, and the pad is removed and thrown away next morning.

The method is not very reliable, but a practicable method that is widely used gives more real help than a more efficient one that people cannot afford.

These, then, are the methods of contraception, using the word in the strict sense. Abortion is not contraception, and neither is abstinence from sex.

There is another method of birth control which is the opposite of contraception; namely action aimed at producing a baby. To affect the husband or wife so that their love-making leads to a birth, is as much birth control as it is to stop them having a child. Curiously, although Marie Stopes herself always stressed this in Constructive Birth Control she entirely ignores it in her large textbook on birth control (perhaps because she thought of birth control and contraception in this book as one and the same thing).

Until satisfactory methods of contraception are devised and accepted, *abortion* is usually the commonest method of birth control, especially in countries where birth control is illegal. Thus in Italy, where abortion and contraception are illegal, *The Times* estimated abortions to be about three million a year in 1971, while live births were under nine hundred thousand. In Japan and many Eastern European countries, abortion was until recently the officially sponsored method of birth control. Where it is legal and properly carried out, there is much less risk to the woman than if the pregnancy is continued to birth, although there may be a slight chance of other complications, which makes contraception a better form of birth control. Properly, abortion should be carried out before the twelfth week of pregnancy.

Opposition to abortion is much greater than to any other method of birth control. Although abortion is now legal in Britain it was illegal and almost universally rejected in the 1920s. The range of opposition to abortion was very widely exploited by those who objected to contraception: many ran all forms of birth control together and condemned all as effectively being abortion.

Abstinence from sex, whether partial or complete, is the only method of birth control approved by the Roman Catholic Church and many other religions. Some moralists still say "The best oral contraceptive is the word NO." This is particularly for the unmarried; for the married, the so-called *safe period* is recommended. This is not true contraception (which means enjoying intercourse without causing a birth). Use of the safe period means going without intercourse at certain periods of the month. Its advantage to the Catholic is that it follows the teachings of the Church. Many non-Catholics would find allowing the calendar to control love-making decidedly unnatural. In any case, this method is far from safe.

Date Chart

1880	15th October, Marie Stopes born in Edinburgh.
1885	First girl's high schools in England.
1885	Louis Pasteur cures rabies.
1892	Marie goes to St. George's School, Edinburgh.
1894	Marie at the North London Collegiate School.
1895	W. Röntgen discovers X-rays.
1898	Marie enters her name to attend University College, London.
1902	Marie graduates from University College as a Bachelor of Science with firstclass honours in botany and geology. Her father, Henry Stopes, dies.
1903	Marie sets off for Munich University and there meets Kuyiro Fujii.
1904	Marie awarded Doctorate of Philosophy at Munich.
1905	Marie gets her first university lectureship at Manchester University.
1907	Marie sets off on a scientific expedition to Japan.
1911	Marie marries Ruggles Gates. Suffragette riots in London.
1914	The marriage to Gates annulled. *Married Love* begun. Outbreak of First World War.
1917	Marie meets H. V. Roe.
1918	Marriage to H. V. Roe. *Married Love* published. Also *Wise Parenthood*. First World War ends. Women over thirty given the vote.
1919	*Letter to Working Mothers* published.

1921	The Queen's Hall meeting.
1923	Marie Stopes sues Dr. Halliday Sutherland for libel. Birth control clinic opens in New York.
1924	Sales of *Married Love* reach half a million.
1925	*First Five Thousand* published. First provincial clinic set up in Wolverhampton.
1926	The General Strike.
1928	Marie Stopes sets up a mobile clinic. Women given the vote on equal terms with men.
1929	*Mother England* published.
1930	*Ten Thousand Cases* published. National Birth Control Council formed.
1933	Marie Stopes resigns from National Birth Control Association.
1939	Beginning of the Second World War. *Love Songs for Young Lovers* published.
1945	Japan, then Germany, surrenders.
1952	The first contraceptive pill introduced.
1958	Marie Stopes dies on 2nd October, aged a few days short of seventy-eight.

Glossary

ABORTION Operation which gets rid of an unborn baby from its mother's womb.

ANGIOSPERMS One of two divisions (the other being *gymnosperms*) of seedbearing plants. The seeds produced by angiosperms are enclosed in capsules.

CAP There are basically three types of cap, each of which prevent *sperm* from reaching the womb to fertilize the egg which may be waiting there. The largest of these, the *diaphragm* or *Dutch cap* covers the cervix and a large part of the vagina. It is made of thin rubber and shaped in the form of a dome with a rim containing a coil spring or flat metal spring. The *cervical cap* or *check pessary* is similar but much smaller and fits snugly over the *cervix.* The *vault cap* is more rigid and fits over the *cervix* and the top end of the *vagina.*

CERVIX The neck of the womb. It is a powerful ring muscle closed at most times but able to expand widely during childbirth.

CHECK PESSARY —see *Cap*

COIL—see *Intra Uterine Device*

COITUS INTERRUPTUS Method of birth control in which the man withdraws his *penis* before reaching a climax so that his *sperm* is spilled outside the vagina.

CONDOM Light rubber sheath unrolled onto the *penis* in which the *sperm* is trapped and prevented from entering the *vagina.*

CYCADS An order of subtropical plant belonging to the *gymnosperms,* looking rather like palms and ferns but botanically very different.

DIAPHRAGM, DUTCH CAP—see *Cap*

GENETIC COUNSELLING An increasingly important part of medicine in which people with a family history of inherited disease (for example haemophilia) are advised about the risk of their children inheriting the disease. In cases where the illness is severe enough to cause handicap to or even death of the child and the risks of inheriting the disease are very high, the advice given may be not to have any children.

GRAFENBERG RINGE An early form of the *intra uterine device* in the form of a silver or silkworm gut ring.

GYMNOSPERMS A division of seedbearing plants. The main feature which distinguishes the *gymnosperms* from the *angiosperms* is that the seeds of the former are not enclosed in capsules.

GYNAECOLOGY Medicine and surgery of the female reproductive system.

INTRA UTERINE DEVICE (I.U.D) An inert foreign body kept in the cavity of the womb which prevents the fertilized egg from developing. Also called the loop or coil, they are nowadays made of plastic, some using a little copper as well.

IN UTERO A Latin phrase meaning, literally, "in the womb."

LOOP—see *Intra Uterine Device*.

MENSTRUATION Periodic bleeding in women of childbearing age which occurs when the womb sheds its lining which has become enriched to prepare for the possible development of a fertilized egg.

NŌ PLAYS An ancient form of Japanese drama.

OBSTETRICS Medical care in pregnancy and childbirth.

ORGASM Climax reached during sexual intercourse.

OVULATION The period of formation of ova (eggs).

PALAEOBOTANY The study of fossil plants.

PENIS Male reproductive organ.

PESSARY Soluble tablet used for getting antiseptics or other drugs into the vagina. It is not to be confused with the *check pessary*.

PILL (ORAL CONTRACEPTIVE) This is a pill which contains certain chemicals which, in the woman, will either stop the egg from being released, stop it being fertilized, or stop it developing in the womb. In the man it will stop sperm being produced or will make them useless. At present the only oral contraceptives generally available are for the woman.

SAFE PERIOD The period between *menstruation* and the next *ovulation,* during which love-making is not likely to result in pregnancy.

SHEATH—see *Condom*

SPERMATOZOA (SPERM) Male germ cells one of which fertilizes the egg in conception. In humans, some two hundred million sperm are released in one orgasm.

SPERMICIDE Chemical which kills sperm.

VAGINA Passage from the external female genitals to the womb.

VASECTOMY This is an operation to prevent sperm being ejected when orgasm is reached. The ducts or tubes from the testicles (balls)—which is where the sperm are produced—are tied.

VIVA VOCE Oral examination.

Index

References to information contained in captions are included in the index

Further Reading

A good full length biography of Marie Stopes is:–
Briant, Keith, *Marie Stopes* (The Hogarth Press, 1962)

Books by Marie Stopes:–
Married Love (Fifield, 1918; The Hogarth Press, 1952)
Contraception: Its Theory, History and Practice (Bale, Sons & Danielsson, 1929)
Our Ostriches (Putnam, 1923)
Love Songs for Young Lovers (Heinemann, 1939)
Wartime Harvest (Alexander Moring, 1944)

Histories of birth control, social histories and modern birth control:–
Wood, Clive, and Suiters, Beryl, *The Fight for Acceptance: History of Contraception* (Medical and Technical, 1970)
Wood, Clive *Birth Control Now and Tomorrow* (Peter Davies, 1969; Corgi, 1971)
Chesney, Kellow, *Victorian Underworld* (M. T. Smith, 1970; Pelican, 1971)
Grave, Robert and Hodge, Alan, *The Long Weekend* (Faber & Faber, 1940)
Hopkins, Harry, *The New Look* (Secker & Warburg, 1963)
Seaman, L. C. B., *Life in Great Britain between the Wars* (Batsford, 1970)

Picture Credits

The author and publisher thank all those who have lent, or given permission for reproduction of, the pictures which appear on the following pages:—Tom Blau, Camera Press: 76; David Low Trustees: 65; International Planned Parenthood Federation: 8 top, 38, 47, 81, 84, 85, 86, 87; Japan Information Centre: 29; Keystone Press: 83; Marie Stopes Memorial Centre: 42, 51, 61, 62, 63, 74, 79; Mary Evans Picture Library: 10 left, 13, 15, 18, 26 bottom, 27 bottom; National Portrait Gallery: 41; Radio Times Hulton Picture Library: 21, 22, 36, 37, 39, 48. The remaining pictures are the property of the author or the Wayland Picture Library.
The author and publisher also thank the Royal Society of Literature for their kind permission to reproduce certain extracts from Marie Stopes' poetry.